NEXT STEPS

A New Believers
Handbook

30 day devotional

Next Steps
A New Believers Handbook

30 day devotional

Dr. Brian Kiley Callaway

Next Steps
New Believers Handbook
30 day devotional

ISBN-13: 978-1492846369

ISBN-10: 1492846368

All Scripture quotations are taken from the New International Version of the Bible.

Printed by CreateSpace

Contents

Welcome to the New Believers Guide

The New Believers Guide was created to take the new or recommitted believer on a journey of discovery and spiritual growth. This guide covers six core principles:

- Knowing God
- Life in the Spirit
- Prayer
- The Bible
- Community
- Sharing Your Faith

Each principle has five lessons which contain Bible passages, thought questions and applications for everyday life.

We want to encourage you to complete all 30 lessons in the order they are presented. We recommend one lesson a day. Take your time, answer all the questions and use these lessons as an opportunity to focus on your relationship with God.

IT IS TIME TO BEGIN! Start each lesson with a brief prayer and ask God to reveal Himself to you through your studies.

1

KNOWING GOD

You Can Be Sure

Day One: Lesson 1

How can you be sure that you have accepted Christ?

A true Christian is someone who believes in God and has asked Jesus Christ, the Son of God, to be their Lord and Savior. God sent His Son Jesus Christ into the world to die for our sins. All of us have done, said or thought things that are wrong. These are called sins and we deserve to be punished for them. The good news is God sent His Son Jesus Christ to die on the cross for our sins.

When you sincerely ask Jesus Christ to be your Lord and Savior and to forgive your sins, you are accepting Christ as your Savior.

The Bible says "As many as received Him, to them He gave the right to become children of God, even to those who believe on His name." So when you accept Christ as your Savior, you become a child of God. Your sins are forgiven and God says you have the gift of eternal life in heaven. You can thank God every day for His wonderful gift of new life in Jesus Christ. You are not a Christian because you are perfect, because in this life we unfortunately will not be perfect. You are not a Christian because you go to church, although you should definitely go to church if you can. But you are a Christian because you have sincerely asked Jesus Christ to be your Lord and Savior and have asked forgiveness for your sins. God loves you and wants you to be His child now and forever.

Journal any thoughts below:

Scriptures

"For God so loved the world, that He gave His only begotten Son, that whoever believes in Him shall not perish, but have eternal life." **John 3: 16**

"But as many as received Him, to them He gave the right to become children of God, even to those who believe in His name, who were born, not of blood nor of the will of the flesh nor of the will of man, but of God."
John 1: 12,13

"This is eternal life, that they may know You, the only true God, and Jesus Christ whom You have sent." **John 17: 3**

How confident are you that you are a Christian?

a. Very
b. Some
c. Little
d. None

Who is God?

Who is God?

God is the Supreme Being who created the heavens and the earth. "In the beginning God created the heavens and the earth." God is invisible; He is a Spirit. God is eternal; He has been from all eternity; He has no beginning and no end. God has all power and all authority. There is no power in heaven or on earth that has more power than God. God is all wise and all knowing; He knows everything and He has perfect wisdom. Picture the wisest and powerful person on earth; then multiply it times a million and you still only have a tiny picture of a little fraction of who God is.

The good news is this all powerful God is loving and kind.

The Bible says God is patient; He is "compassionate and gracious, slow to anger, abounding in love." He cares for us just like a perfect and wonderful father would care for his own children. God loves us and is ready to forgive our sins when we sincerely ask Jesus Christ to be our Savior. God knows what is best for us; He will lead and guide us with His loving eyes on us. And most wonderful of all, He is ready to spend all eternity with us in heaven when we truly have accepted Jesus Christ. God has prepared a wonderful place for us in heaven forever.

Journal any thoughts below:

Scriptures

"In the beginning God created the heavens and the earth."
Genesis 1: 1

"For as high as the heavens are above the earth, so great is His (God's) loving-kindness toward those who fear Him. As far as the east is from the west, So far has He removed our transgressions from us." **Psalm 103: 11,12**

"All authority has been given to Me in heaven and on earth." (Jesus speaking) **Matthew 28: 18**

How powerful and loving is God?

How certain are you that God loves you and He knows what is best for your life?

a. Very
b. Some
c. Little
d. None

Knowing Jesus

New Believers Guide: Lesson 3

Who is Jesus?

Jesus is the Son of God who came to earth in human form. 2,000 years ago, God sent His Son Jesus Christ to be born of a virgin in the country Israel. The Bible explains that Jesus existed with God in heaven before He came down to earth as a man. This is because Jesus is part of the Godhead, which includes God the Father, Jesus Christ, and the Holy Spirit. These are 3 persons, but one God. John 1:1-4 says this about Jesus: "In the beginning the Word already existed. The Word was with God, and the Word was God. He existed in the beginning with God. God created everything through him, and nothing was created except through him. The Word gave life to everything that was created, and his life brought light to everyone."

Jesus lived on this earth for 33 years.

He performed many miracles and He taught about God. His teachings are contained in the Bible in the books of Matthew, Mark, Luke and John. Jesus lives a perfect life without sin. When He was 33 years old Jesus was killed; He died on a cross which was an execution for common criminals. He willingly gave Himself to die to pay the penalty for our sins.

The Bible teaches that Jesus is both fully human and fully God.

Listen to what Philippians 2:6-10 tells us about Him: "Although He [Christ] existed in the form of God, did not regard equality with God a thing to be grasped, but emptied Himself, taking the form of a bond-servant, and being make in the likeness of men. Being found in appearance as a man, He humbled Himself by becoming obedient to the point of death, even death on a cross. For this reason also, God highly exalted Him, and bestowed on Him the name which is above every name, so that at the name of Jesus every knee will bow, of those who are in heaven and on earth and under the earth." Wow, what a powerful description of Jesus! This is why we worship Him as the Savior and Lord of the universe.

Jesus came from the Father and was born of a virgin, performed many miracles, and foretold of His death and resurrection.

When God raised Him from the dead, it proved that Jesus is who He said He is—the very Son of God and Savior of the world. After His resurrection, Jesus returned to his position in Heaven where He now reigns with God and prays for those who believe in Him. We will meet Him again at His Second Coming and live with Him in heaven for eternity. How wonderful that will be! Take a moment and honor Jesus as the Lord of all and your Savior and friend. Ask Him to reveal Himself more to you.

Journal any thoughts below:

Scriptures

"I am the way, and the truth, and the life; no one comes to the Father but through Me." **John 14: 6**

"I and the Father are one." **John 10: 30**

"For by Him all things were created, both in the heavens and on earth, visible and invisible, whether thrones or dominions or rulers or authorities—all things have been created through Him and for Him." **Colossians 1: 16**

Why is Jesus the only way to be made right with God?

How convinced are you that Jesus is God?
a. Very
b. Some
c. Little
d. None

You are Saved by Grace

New Believers Guide: Lesson 4

Everyone is in need of salvation.

The Bible, in Romans 5, tells us that all sin and fall short of God's glory and that this sin deserves death. How many sin? ALL. And since all of us sin, all of us face death. Our sin is what separates us from God, and it only takes one sin. Our good deeds cannot change that. Imagine someone was guilty of murder and was pleading his case in court: "But I fed the homeless, Your Honor! I also gave away money to charity and was nice to my mom!" His few good acts wouldn't erase the murder he had committed. He would still have to pay the penalty for his sin. It is the same with us. Stuck in our sin and moving towards death, all of us are in a hopeless situation.

But here's the good news: God, in His mercy, sent His Son to die in our place.

Ephesians 2:8,9 says, "For by grace you have been saved through faith; and that not of yourselves, it is the gift of God; not as a result of works, so that no one may boast." Christ paid the penalty for our sins by dying in our place as a totally innocent man. Like a bridge, connecting two separated people, God made a way through Christ to connect us to Himself. God did that because He wanted to—not because He had to—because of His great love for us. This is the grace of God, and it is given to us by faith in His Son Jesus, not by working hard to be good. Isn't that a relief? Take a moment and thank God for saving you while you were still a sinner. Thank Him that you don't have to earn His love or salvation.

Journal any thoughts below:

Scriptures

"But we believe that we are saved through the grace of the Lord Jesus, in the same way as they also are."
Acts 15: 11

"So that, as sin reigned in death, even so grace would reign through righteousness to eternal life through Jesus Christ our Lord." **Romans 5: 21**

"In Him we have redemption through His blood, the forgiveness of our trespasses, according to the riches of His grace." **Ephesians 1: 7**

According to the Bible, what do you have to do to be saved?

Are you certain you have accepted Christ as your Savior?

a. Very
b. Some
c. Little
d. None

God Created You for a Purpose

Have you ever wondered why you were born?

Augustine, one of the early church fathers, said "Our hearts are restless until we find God." You cannot truly experience peace and joy in your life without an open relationship with God. Romans 5:1,2 tells us, "Therefore, having been justified by faith, we have peace with God through our Lord Jesus Christ, through whom also we have obtained our introduction by faith into this grace in which we stand; and we exult in hope of the glory of God."

The purpose of your life is to bring God glory in everything you do: in your worship, your relationships, and your work.

"The chief purpose of man in to bring glory and honor to God and to enjoy Him forever," says the Westminster Confession of Faith. Remember, by accepting Christ as your Savior you now have God who "is at work in you, both to will and to work for His good pleasure" (Philippians 2:13). But this does not happen overnight. It is the result of a growing relationship with God. Faithfulness to read God's Word and to pray according to His will help grow your relationship with God. That is the ultimate purpose of your life—to have a meaningful relationship with God. And beyond that, God has specific things for you to accomplish in your life. The next section deals with the special plan God has for your life. Take a moment and thank God that He knows you and cares for you specifically and has a great plan for your life.

Journal any thoughts below:

Scriptures

"But, indeed, for this reason I have allowed you to remain, in order to show you My power and in order to proclaim My name through all the earth." **Exodus 9: 16**

"I cry out to God Most High, To God who accomplishes all things for me." **Psalm 57: 2**

"And I will give them one heart and one way, that they may fear Me always, for their own good and for the good of their children after them." **Jeremiah 32: 39**

Based on what you have seen so far, why do you think God created you?

I am confident that God has a plan for my life.

a. Very
b. Some
c. Little
d. None

The Holy Spirit

Who is the Holy Spirit? And what does He have to do with your life?

You received the Spirit the moment you accepted Christ as your Savior, and He will never leave you. Ephesians 1:13 says, "You were sealed in Him with the Holy Spirit of promise." Have you ever put a label on something to show others it is yours? When you became a Christian, God put a stamp on you, claiming you as redeemed and forgiven. That stamp is His own Spirit. And this Holy Spirit is your greatest friend and helper in life. He prays for you, helps you deal with the challenges of life, and is the power that transforms your life. Think of it this way: before we accepted Christ we were like a light bulb without electricity. But now, the Holy Spirit is the "electricity" that lights up our lives.

The Spirit gives you a whole new life.

Jesus, in John 6:63, says, "It is the Spirit who gives life; the flesh profits nothing; the words that I have spoken to you are spirit and are life." The Bible talks about being "born again." What that means is simply that the Spirit has given you a fresh start and an entirely new nature to live differently. Galatians 2:20 says, "I have been crucified with Christ; and it is no longer I who live, but Christ lives in me; and the LIFE which I now live in the flesh I live by faith in the Son of

God, who loved me and gave Himself up for me." It's like a car that was constantly breaking down, and someone came and put in an entirely new engine. If you are a Christian, you already have the Holy Spirit living inside of you; now you just need to learn how to relate with Him and walk in the new life He has for you. Read on in the next lessons about what exactly the Holy Spirit does to change your life and how to receive His power and grace.

Journal any thoughts below:

Scriptures

"It will come about after this That I will pour out My Spirit on all mankind; And your sons and daughters will prophesy, Your old men will dream dreams, Your young men will see visions." **Joel 2: 28**

"I baptize you with water for repentance, but He who is coming after me is mightier than I, and I am not fit to remove His sandals; He will baptize you with the Holy Spirit and fire." **Matthew 3: 11**

"In Him, you also, after listening to the message of truth, the gospel of your salvation—having also believed, you were sealed in Him with the Holy Spirit of promise, who is given as a pledge of our inheritance, with a view to the redemption of God's own possession, to the praise of His glory." **Ephesians 1: 13,14**

What does it mean to you to have the power of the Holy Spirit in your life?

How often are your thoughts/actions changed by a prompting from God's Spirit?

a. rarely
b. weekly
c. daily

2
LIFE IN
THE SPIRIT

How You Can Be Filled With the Holy Spirit

We are given the gift of the Holy Spirit when we truly ask Jesus Christ to be our Savior and to forgive our sins. But it is our choice whether we are truly filled, and controlled, and empowered by the Holy Spirit. Think of it like this. You may have a King who comes to live in your house. You can ask him to live in a small room; or you can ask him to be in charge of the whole house. So you can have the Holy Spirit in your life but you can try to run your own life, or you can ask God the Holy Spirit to fill and control your entire life.

To ask the Holy Spirit to fill and control and empower your **life**, and to fill you with God's love and power, you can pray and ask in faith for God to fill you with His Holy Spirit. Here is a sample prayer that you can pray. "Holy Father, thank You that You gave Your Son Jesus Christ to die on the cross for my sins. I ask forgiveness for my sins and want You to be Lord over my life and to be in control. I give You control of my life and ask that you fill and control me with Your Holy Spirit. Please be in charge of my life every day and give me Your power to live a Christian life each and every day."

Journal any thoughts below:

Scriptures

"For the law of the Spirit of life in Christ Jesus has set you free from the law of sin and of death." **Romans 8:2**

"However, you are not in the flesh but in the Spirit, if indeed the Spirit of God dwells in you. But if anyone does not have the Spirit of Christ, he does not belong to Him." **Romans 8:9**
"But I say, walk by the Spirit, and you will not carry out the desire of the flesh." **Galatians 5:16**

Have I really committed my life to be filled and controlled by God's Holy Spirit?

Are you aware of the Holy Spirit's leading in your life?
a. very
b. some
c. little
d. none

The Holy Spirit's Work in Your Life

The Holy Spirit is your constant companion and helper.

Have you ever been given a task that is too big for you? Living like Jesus is impossible for us on our own. But that's why God gave us His own Spirit—to help us live as new people. Jesus said, "But the Helper, the Holy Spirit, whom the Father will send in My name, He will teach you all things, and bring to your remembrance all that I said to you" (John 14:26). As we saw in the last lesson, the Spirit is the stamp of God's salvation and gives us new life. But He does a lot more. Let's look at the things He does for you:

The Spirit teaches.

Do you ever wonder HOW to live the Christian life? 2 Timothy 3:16 tells us, "All Scripture is inspired by God and profitable for teaching." "Inspired by God" is a reference to the Holy Spirit who is the life-giving breath of God. It's like studying a book and having the author of the book there with you to help you through the hard-to-understand parts. Since the Holy Spirit inspired the Bible, He will help you to understand it and give you new life as you read it.

The Spirit corrects.

2 Timothy 3:16 also tells us another benefit of the Holy Spirit: He corrects us. "All Scripture is inspired by God and is useful for teaching, for showing people what is wrong in their lives, for correcting faults, and for teaching us how to live right." As believers, we will experience the prompting of the Spirit in our lives when we do things that God does not want us to do. For example, sometimes we may not want to forgive someone for wronging us. The Spirit will keep reminding us of the importance of forgiving that person and how God has forgiven us.

The Spirit leads.

John 16:13 tells us, "But when He, the Spirit of truth, comes, He will guide you into all truth; for He will not speak on His own initiative, but whatever He hears, He will speak; and He will disclose to you what is to come." When you follow the leading of the Spirit, you follow God's will for your life. Sometimes we resist the Spirit and do things of our own will and not God's. To be self-willed only delays God's blessing in our lives. The Bible tells us we must decrease the control we have over our lives and turn control over to the leading of the Spirit. This will lead to living the abundant life God has for you.

Journal any thoughts below:

Scriptures

"For who among men knows the thoughts of a man except the spirit of the man which is in him? Even so the thoughts of God no one knows except the Spirit of God." **I Corinthians 2:11**

"But the Helper, the Holy Spirit, whom the Father will send in My name, He will teach you all things, and bring to your remembrance all that I said to you." **John 14:26**

"I will ask the Father, and He will give you another Helper, that He may be with you forever; that is the Spirit of truth, whom the world cannot receive, because it does not see Him or know Him, but you know Him because He abides with you and will be in you." **John 14:16,17**

What do I need to do to turn more control of my life over to the Holy Spirit?

I am confident that the Holy Spirit is working in my life.
a. very
b. some
c. little
d. none

The Holy Spirit's Power

New Believers Guide: Lesson 9

How much power does the Holy Spirit have?

The Spirit has all the power of God because He is God. The life-giving power of the Spirit is seen at creation. We are told in Genesis 1:2 that the "Spirit of God was moving over the surface of the waters" and that God said, "Let us make man in OUR likeness" (Genesis 1:26), demonstrating the equality of the God and the Spirit. We receive the POWER of the Holy Spirit the moment we receive Christ. Romans 8:11 says, "But if the Spirit of Him who raised Jesus from the dead dwells in you, He who raised Christ Jesus from the dead will also give life to your mortal bodies through His Spirit who dwells in you."

What kind of power does the Holy Spirit give?

Paul tells us two important things. The Spirit gives us the power to love others as God loves us and to be witnesses for Jesus. Jesus said, "But you will receive power when the Holy Spirit has come upon you; and you shall be My witnesses both in Jerusalem, and in all Judea and Samaria, and even to the remotest part of the earth." (Acts 1:8).

Where do we begin to access this power?

We begin by asking God to fill us with His Spirit and confessing areas where we have ignored God. Jesus said, "how much more will your heavenly Father give the Holy Spirit to those who ask Him?" (Luke 11:13). Ask the Holy Spirit today to help you love others as God does and be a great witness to Jesus in the world. You will begin to experience the abundant life God has for you as you do.

Journal any thoughts below:

Scriptures

"Then he breathed on them and said, "Receive the Holy Spirit. If you forgive anyone's sins, they are forgiven. If you do not forgive them, they are not forgiven." **John 20:22,23**

"But you will receive power when the Holy Spirit comes upon you. And you will be my witnesses, telling people about me everywhere—in Jerusalem, throughout Judea, in Samaria, and to the ends of the earth." **Acts 1:8**

"After this prayer, the meeting place shook, and they were all filled with the Holy Spirit. Then they preached the word of God with boldness." **Acts 4:31**

Who do you need to forgive? Who can you pray for to receive Christ?

I am certain of the Holy Spirit's presence in my life.
a. very
b. some
c. little
d. none

Living in the Spirit

New Believers Guide: Lesson 10

What kind of life do you want?

Jesus makes a promise to us in John 10:10: "I come that they have life and have it to the full." We can claim that promise by living life in the Spirit. In the last lesson we learned that life is a battle between our sinful nature and our spiritual nature. Paul teaches us a great lesson in Galatians 6:7,8: "People harvest only what they plant. If they plant to satisfy their sinful selves, their sinful selves will bring them ruin. But if they plant to please the Spirit, they will receive eternal life from the Spirit." Think of yourself as a farmer and your life as a crop. What do you want to grow in your life? If we sow seeds of selfish desires, we grow a crop that reflects that.

However, we can sow seeds according to the spirit and have a crop that produces wonderful, spiritual fruit.

Listen to Paul describe that difference between the two kinds of lifestyles in Galatians 5: "Now the deeds of the flesh are evident, which are: immorality, impurity, sensuality, idolatry, sorcery, enmities, strife, jealousy, outbursts of anger, disputes, dissensions, factions, envying, drunkenness, carousing, and things like these, of which I forewarn you, just as I have forewarned you, that those who practice such things will not inherit the kingdom of God. But the fruit of the Spirit is love, joy, peace, patience, kindness, goodness, faithfulness, gentleness, self-control; against such things there is no law."

What kind of crops do you want to harvest in your life?

Ask the Holy Spirit to fill you right now and help you to sow according to His way. He wants to bless your life and produce good fruit. You just need to trust and obey Him.

Journal any thoughts below:

Scriptures

"For those who are according to the flesh set their minds on the things of the flesh, but those who are according to the Spirit, the things of the Spirit. For the mind set on the flesh is death, but the mind set on the Spirit is life and peace." **Romans 8:5,6**

"Do not grieve the Holy Spirit of God, by whom you were sealed for the day of redemption." **Ephesians 4:30**

"Now the Lord is the Spirit, and where the Spirit of the Lord is, there is liberty. But we all, with unveiled face, beholding as in a mirror the glory of the Lord, are being transformed into the same image from glory to glory, just as from the Lord, the Spirit."
2 Corinthians 3: 17,18

What type of crop do I want to see in my life 10 years from now?

To what extent do you want to hand over more control of your life to the Holy Spirit?
a. Very
b. Some
c. Little
d. None

3
PRAYER

What is Prayer?

What is prayer?

Prayer is the ability to communicate with your Heavenly Father and hear back from Him! Some think of it as a duty. Others think of it as a quick fix or last resort. Prayer is none of these things. It is actually the greatest privilege of a Christian. The whole Bible is filled with the command to pray: "Pray in the morning", "Pray when you are sick", "Pray when you need help", "Pray for peace." Why are we told to pray so much? It is because God wants to answer our requests. Jesus said, "And all things you ask in prayer, believing, you will receive" (Matthew 21:22). What a promise!

Think about your relationship with your best friend.

You talk to him, listen to what he has to say, and enjoy spending time together. This is the essence of prayer, building a relationship with your Heavenly Father. He loves you very much, wants to hear what is on your mind and give you direction. God says, "Call to Me and I will answer you, and I will tell you great and mighty things, which you do not know" (Jeremiah 33:3). Your job is to call out and talk to Him, and He promises to answer—what a wonderful guarantee! Your prayers do not have to be anything fancy. In fact, God prefers honesty over babbling on and on. Just start today by telling God what is on your mind and asking Him to speak to you. You will be amazed at His response.

Journal any thoughts below:

Scriptures

"I have called upon You, for You will answer me, O God; Incline Your ear to me, hear my speech." **Psalm 17:6**

"WHEN YOU SAID, "'Seek My face,'" my heart said to You, "'Your face, O LORD, I shall seek." **Psalm 27:8**

"This is the confidence which we have before Him, that, if we ask anything according to His will, He hears us. And if we know that He hears us IN whatever we ask, we know that we have the requests which we have asked from Him." **I John 5:14-15**

Why do you think God wants you to pray?

How satisfied are you with your daily prayer life?

a. Very

b. Little

c. Not

Why Pray?

What is the point of prayer?

Why take time out of your day to talk with God who you can't see or necessarily hear out loud? The main reason we pray is because it's what God wants. Why does God want you to call out to Him? Think of the relationship between a father and son. A good father wants his son to come to him with his feelings and needs; it is his desire to provide for his son and let him know he can be trusted. This is even truer of God! Listen to what Jesus said about praying to God: "Or what man is there among you who, when his son asks for a loaf, will give him a stone? Or if he asks for a fish, he will not give him a snake, will he? If you then, being evil, know how to give good gifts to your children, how much more will your Father who is in heaven give what is good to those who ask Him! (Matthew 7:9-11).

Have you ever had a friend who wants to hear about your problems? Probably not. But it makes God happy when you talk to Him about your thoughts and needs, because it shows Him that you trust Him. The Bible says, "And without faith it is impossible to please Him, for he who comes to God must believe that He is and that He is a rewarder of those who seek Him" (Hebrews 11:6). Faith just means that you believe God is who He says He is in the Bible. For example, you can ask God what to do in a certain situation and believe He will guide you because James 1:5 says, "But if any of you lacks wisdom, let him ask of God, who gives to all generously and without reproach, and it will be given to him." Why don't you take some time today to tell God a pressing need or thought that has been weighing you down? Relying on your Heavenly Father will both please Him and build your faith as you see Him respond to your request.

Journal any thoughts below:

Scriptures

"The LORD has heard my supplication, The LORD receives my prayer." **Psalm 6:9**

"Be anxious for nothing, but in everything by prayer and supplication with thanksgiving let your requests be made known to God. And the peace of God, which surpasses all comprehension, will guard your hearts and your minds in Christ Jesus." **Philippians 4:6,7**

"Is anyone among you suffering? Then he must pray. Is anyone cheerful? He is to sing praises." **James 5:13**

When you are worried about something, what does the Bible say you should do?

How often do you pray about the needs in your life?

a. Often

b. Sometimes

c. Not often

d. Never

When to Pray

Have you ever needed something really badly from the store and found it closed?

It used to be that many stores were closed on Sundays. If you needed something, you would just have to wait until Monday to get it. God is not like that. His ears are always open to hear what you have to say. The Bible says, "He will not allow your foot to slip; He who keeps you will not slumber. Behold, he who keeps Israel will neither slumber nor sleep." (Psalm 121:3,4). You can know that you can come to God at any time and have His full attention. And your prayers don't have to be especially long. You can shoot up an "arrow" prayer to God anytime: "God I need your peace," or "Please comfort me right now." He loves you that much.

But how much should you pray?

Should you pray every hour on the hour or just once a week? The Bible does not give a specific amount to pray. Instead, it tells us to pray continually. Paul said, "Rejoice always; pray without ceasing; in everything, give thanks, for this is God's will for you in Christ Jesus" (1 Thess. 5:16-18). Does this mean you can't ever sleep? No, no: Think of prayer like water. Health experts tell us to drink water continually. This doesn't mean you have to drink water at all moments of the day; the point is to stay hydrated by frequently drinking water. It's the same with prayer. You can keep spiritually hydrated by communicating with God throughout the day, telling Him your needs, asking him for guidance, and thanking Him for all of His many blessings. You can talk to Him at work, while you drive in the car, even when you are talking with other people! Practice close communication with God today and see the difference that it makes.

Journal any thoughts below:

Scriptures

"Devote yourselves to prayer keeping alert in it with an attitude of thanksgiving." **Colossians 4:2**

"It will also come to pass that before they call, I will answer; and while they are still speaking, I will hear." **Isaiah 65:24**

"Evening and morning and at noon, I will complain and murmur, and He will hear my voice." **Psalm 55:17**

What changes can you make to increase the amount of time you spend praying to God?

How much time are you spending each day in prayer with God?
a. Little or none
b. 5 minutes or less
c. more than 10 minutes

Where to Pray

Prayer can happen anytime, anywhere.

Have you ever had a cell phone conversation cut off because you lost your signal? That will never happen with prayer, because God's Spirit is everywhere and even lives inside of you! 2 Chronicles 16:9 says, "For the eyes of the LORD move to and fro throughout the earth, the He may strongly support those whose heart is completely His..." So wherever you are—whether it's the grocery store, your room, or your job—God always hears you.

Jesus knew this better than anyone else.

He said, "Father, thank you for hearing me. I know you always hear me" (John 11:42). As a Christian, you have the same assurance as Jesus to know that God hears your every prayer. This is a great source of comfort, as God is never more than a prayer away. He is ready to hear you at all times, but sometimes to hear clearly from Him, you have to go somewhere without distraction. Have you ever tried to have an important conversation with a friend in a very loud restaurant? Not easy. Just the same, often we need to find a quiet place to pray and connect with God. Listen to what Jesus did: "It was very early in the morning, while it was still dark. Jesus got up, left the house, and went away to a secluded place and was praying there"

(Mark 1:35). Do you have a special place you can meet with God? If not, find a place to get away from the noise of your life and spend time there with God today. You will feel refreshed and find it easier to connect with God.

Journal any thoughts below:

Scriptures

"The LORD is far from the wicked, but he hears the prayers of the righteous."
Proverbs 15: 29

"With all prayer and petition pray at all times in the Spirit and with this in view be on alert with all perseverance and petition for all the saints." **Ephesians 6:18**

"It was at this time that He went off to the mountain to pray and He spent the whole night in prayer to God" **Luke 6:12**

Do you have a quite place you can go to be alone with God?

How often do you take time out to spend quality time with God alone daily?

a. More than an hour

b. 30 minutes

c. 15 minutes or less

d. Never

How to Pray

Is there a right way to pray?

Jesus' disciples were wondering this when they said, "Lord, teach us how to pray" (Luke 11:1). Upon being asked, Jesus gave His disciples—us—a model prayer. It goes like this: "Our Father, who is in heaven, Hallowed be Your name. Your kingdom come Your will be done, on earth as it is in heaven. Give us this day our daily bread. And forgive us for our debts, as we also have forgiven our debtors. And do not lead us into temptation, but deliver us from evil. For Yours is the Kingdom and the power and the glory forever, Amen." (Matthew 6:9-13). Why this prayer? Jesus didn't mean that this would be the only words you could pray. Otherwise He wouldn't have prayed other things He did in the Bible. Instead, this prayer guides us, just as railroad tracks guide a train. Look at the different parts of the prayer:

Our Father, who is in heaven, Hallowed be your name: You can praise God for His great name and who He is.

Your kingdom come your will be done, on earth as it is in heaven: You can ask God to take control of your circumstances.

Give us this day our daily bread: You can ask God for whatever you need.

Forgive us our debts as we also forgive our debtors: You can receive forgiveness from God for your sins and forgive those who have hurt you.

And do not lead us into temptation, but deliver us from evil: You can ask for God's protection against Satan and sin.

For yours is the Kingdom and the power and the glory forever, Amen: You can get an eternal perspective and rely on God for everything.

What is the recipe for great prayer?

Have you ever tried to make a cake without flour? The cake would fall flat because it has no substance. Faith is the substance of prayer. You can add in all the ingredients of the Lord's Prayer, but if you don't have faith in God, they won't do much good. Jesus said, "Have faith in God. Truly I say to you, whoever says to this mountain, 'Be taken up and cast into the sea,' and does not doubt in his heart, but believes that what he says is going to happen, it will be granted him" (Mark 11:22,23). How do you have faith in God? Basically, you just believe what God says in the Bible is true. Say you told your child, "I want you to help you get good grades." He would know that if he needed help studying, he could come to you for help. It's just like that with God: Whatever He has promised in the Bible you can trust He will do. Why don't you take some time today and pray through the Lord's Prayer and believe that God will give you what you ask for in Jesus' name.

Journal any thoughts below:

Scriptures

"Ask, and it will be given to you; seek, and you will find; knock, and it will be opened to you. For everyone who asks receives, and he who seeks finds, and to him who knocks it will be opened."
Matthew 7: 7,8

"If you believer, you will receive whatever you ask for in prayer."
Matthew 21:22

"In the same way, the Spirit helps us in our weakness. We do not know what we ought to pray for, but the Spirit himself intercedes for us with groans that words can not express." **Romans 8:26**

What did you learn from the Lord's Prayer that will change the way you pray?

As a result of these prayer lessons, how would you rate your daily prayer experience?

a. Very good

b. Good

c. So-so

d. Not good

4

THE BIBLE

What is the Bible?

Where did the Bible come from? The Bible is God's Holy Word. It is inspired by God and can guide you to new life in Jesus Christ and teach you how to live a Godly life. It was written over a period of 1600 years, by more than forty different writers, on three different continents, and in three different languages—and every book of the Bible has a unified message and points us to God. Timothy 3:16 says, "All Scripture is God-breathed." When it says "God-breathed", it means that the Spirit of God inspired the writers to write what God wanted us to know. This fact is confirmed by the Spirit within us which testifies to the truth in the Bible. Hebrews 4:12 says, "For the word of God is alive and powerful." In other words, the unique "living" feature of the Bible is confirmed as it speaks personally to you. Scripture has the power to transform our lives and feed our souls.

How is the Bible organized? The Bible contains 66 Books: 39 in the Old Testament and 27 in the New Testament. Testament simply means covenant, a word that refers to God's promises to us and His faithfulness to honor those promises. Each book has a different theme and a different way of showing who God is and teaching us His ways. Have you ever had someone teach you a point using many different illustrations? That's how the Bible is: there are so many different stories and ways God shows us who He is and who we are. Talking about the things that happened to people in Bible, it says, "These things happened to them as examples and were written down as warnings for us, on whom the fulfilment of the ages has come." (1 Corinthians 10:11). We can learn from the things people went through in the Bible and feel comforted by them. Take a moment and thank God He gave us so many stories and ways to understand Him.

Journal any thoughts below:

Scriptures

"Your word is a lamp to guide my feet and a light for my path."
Psalm 119:105

"The grass withers and the flowers fall, but the word of our God stands forever.." **Isaiah 40:8**

"For the word of God is living and active. Sharper than any double-edged sword, it penetrates even to dividing soul and spirit, joints and marrow; it judges the thoughts and attitudes of the heart."
Hebrews 4:12

How do I know the Bible is the word of God?

How confident are you that the Bible is God's Word?

a. Very

b. Some

c. Little

d. None

The Power of the Bible in Your Life

New Believers Guide: Lesson 17

God's Word the Bible can have tremendous power in your life.

In accepting Jesus Christ as your Savior, you have begun a new life in Jesus Christ. There are some key ways that God's Word the Bible can help transform your life. First, the Bible can teach you about salvation and about new life in Jesus Christ. You can be sure of your salvation. Second, the Bible can help you grow in your faith. "Faith comes by hearing, and hearing by the Word of God."

Third, **the Bible can give you spiritual power over evil**. Even Jesus Christ, when He was tempted, quoted the Bible and displayed power and victory. The Bible is "The sword of the Spirit which is the Word of God." Fourth, the Bible can teach you how to live. "Your Word is a lamp to my feet and a light to my path." Fifth, the Bible can show you in your own life, what is good and what is not good. Often we are blind to our own faults; just like in the dark you cannot tell the difference between a bright shirt and a dark shirt. The Bible "judges the thoughts and attitudes of the heart." And sixth, you can use the Bible to help others. God wants us to be victorious over sin and evil. "God has not given us the spirit of fear, but of power and love and a sound mind." God has given you tremendous spiritual power through faith in His Holy Word.

Journal any thoughts below:

Scriptures

"Do good to your servant according to your word, O Lord."
Psalm 119:65

"Your commands make me wiser than my enemies, for they are ever with me." **Psalm 119:98**

"Long ago I learned from your statutes that You established them to last forever." **Psalm 119:152**

How often do you use the Bible as a measuring rod to help you make decisions in your life?

How often are you sharing things you learn in the Bible with others?

a. Often

b. Sometimes

c. Not often

d. Never

How to Read the Bible

New Believers Guide: Lesson 18

How do you read the Bible?

Is there one right way? Sometimes it can be a bit difficult to start reading the Bible on your own since the names of the books, people, and places are not familiar to us. Here are a few facts to help get you started: The Bible is divided into two parts—the Old Testament and the New Testament. The Old Testament covers the history of Israel's relationship with God and looks forward to God sending Jesus as Savior. The New Testament begins with the coming of Jesus in the first four books (called The Gospels), followed by the letters which tell us how to now live as Christians. Since Christ is the focus of both the Old and the New Testament, a great place to start your reading is with one of the four Gospels—Matthew, Mark, Luke, or John.

The rest of the Bible is for your benefit too.

Joshua 1:8 says, "Study this Book of Instruction continually. Meditate on it day and night so you will be sure to obey everything written in it. Only then will you prosper and succeed in all you do." It is filled with answers to your questions about life and God, and God can speak personally to you through it. Remember, God has given the Holy Spirit as your teacher and He will be your guide as you read the words He inspired. Paul tells us in Romans 8:16, "The Spirit Himself testifies within our spirit." Why don't you start reading the Bible every day? You can start in one of the Gospels in the New Testament, and ask God to speak to you about Jesus. God wants to open your mind to understand His word and change you into His image as you read it. Try to dedicate 15 minutes a day to reading the Bible and see what God does in your life.

Journal any thoughts below:

Scriptures

"When your words came, I ate them; they were my joy and my heart's delight, for I bear your name, O Lord God Almighty." **Jeremiah 15:16**

"Jesus replied, "Blessed rather are those who hear the word of God and obey it." **Luke 11:28**

"Therefore, get rid of all moral filth and the evil that is so prevalent and humbly accept the word planted in you, which can save you." **James 1:21**

Why is it important for you to have time set aside each day to read the Bible?

How important is it for a Christian to read the Bible?

a. Very

b. Some

c. Little

d. None

The Bible is Trustworthy

New Believers Guide: Lesson 19

How do you know you can trust the Bible?

Can you believe it as God's very words to you? Listen to what the Bible says about itself: "All Scripture is inspired by God..." (2 Timothy 3:16). Additionally, every book of the Old Testament is quoted in the New Testament. Jesus often quoted from the Old Testament as did Paul and the other Apostles. Even greater evidence for the authenticity of the Bible is its power to change lives. When someone asked Dr. Ironsides how he knew the Bible is not just another book, he said, "For everyone one person you bring whose life has been transformed by another book, I will bring 100 who have been transformed by the Bible." Millions of changed lives testify to the power of the Bible.

But how can we know if words weren't added to the Bible over time and aren't reliable?

We know the Bible is reliable for several reasons. Several ancient texts of the Old Testament were found in a cave near the Dead Sea in the 1950's. When these texts were compared with newer ones, the accuracy was near 100%. The same is true of the New Testament as well. Of the more than 5000 existing manuscripts dated from 100 to 500AD, there is a better than 99% correlation. Martin Luther said, "The Bible is a Lion and can defend itself." The Bible has been an international best-selling book for nearly 300 years and its power and trustworthiness are confirmed by its 3000 year history and transformative power. You can trust the Bible as God's very word to your life. Begin to read it as God's communication to you and His guide on how to live your life.

Journal any thoughts below:

Scriptures

"The law of the Lord is perfect, reviving the soul. The statutes of the Lord are trustworthy making wise the simple." **Psalm 19:7**

"All Scripture is God-breathed and is useful for teaching, rebuking, correcting and training in righteousness, so that the man of God may be thoroughly equipped for every good work." **2 Timothy 3:16,17**

"Above all, you must understand that no prophecy of Scripture came about by the prophet's own interpretation. For prophecy never had its origin in the will of men, but spoke from God as they were carried along by the Holy Spirit." **2 Peter 1:20,21**

What have I learned so far about the Bible, and how am I going to use it in my life?

How confident are you that the Bible is trustworthy?

a. Very

b. Some

c. Little

d. None

Developing a Daily Pattern

Have you ever heard the saying, "Practice makes perfect?" Maybe you have tried eating really healthy before. And if you have, you know that the effects don't happen overnight, but have to be continued for a lasting effect. It's the same with reading God's Word. As Christians, it is important for us develop a daily pattern of prayer and Bible study. Then we will see the effects of following God's word throughout our whole lives. The apostle Peter said in II Peter 3:18 that we "should grow in the grace and the knowledge of our Lord and Savior Jesus Christ." Spiritual growth, just like physical growth, requires a source of nutrition. Jesus said He is the "living bread that came down from heaven" (John 6:51) and that whoever "eats this bread will live forever" (John 6:58). So in order for us to receive the benefits of our relationship with God, we have to spend time every day with Him in His word to grow in our faith.

How do we start?

• Set aside time each day: It doesn't have to be a long period, but it helps if the time is consistent, early in the morning before work, for example.

• Pray before you read; ask the Holy Spirit to be your teacher.

• Have some paper and a pencil: Write down what you are learning and read back over your notes as a reminder of what the Spirit is teaching you.

• Put what you read into practice. If you read this morning about loving your enemies, try being kind to those who are mean to you that day.

The most important step is to get started.

A great place to start is in the book of John. Begin by reading the entire book just as you would read a letter from a good friend. After that, go back to the beginning and read one chapter a day for the next 21 days. Your Online Missionary is available to help with any questions that you may have as you read. Send them an email anytime, and don't forget to share with them the things God is teaching you and the joy that comes from a growing relationship with Him. As you read, you will learn so much about Jesus, and God will speak to you.

Journal any thoughts below:

Scriptures

"For everything that was written in the past was written to teach us, so that through endurance and the encouragement of the Scriptures we might have hope." **Romans 15:4**

"And how from infancy you have known the holy Scriptures, which are able to make you wise for salvation through faith in Christ Jesus." **2 Timothy 3:15**

"Take the helmet of salvation and the sword of the Spirit, which is the word of God." **Ephesians 6:17**

When would be a good time for you to schedule in reading the Bible in your daily routine?

How often do you read your Bible?

a. Seldom

b. One or two times a week

c. Daily

5
COMMUNITY

When you became a Christian, you joined a family

When you became a Christian, you joined a family.

"What's the difference?" you say. A lot. You can change your religion, but you can't change your family. Your family is with you for life: through good and bad, thick or thin. Your family shapes who you are. The Bible says, "Yet to all who received him, to those who believed in his name, He gave the right to become children of God—children born not of natural descent, nor of human decision or a husband's will, but born of God" (John 1:12).

This family is called "The Church".

And it is the most beautiful group of people on earth: God's own children given the amazing privilege of showing the world who He is. I Peter 2:9-10 says, "But you are a chosen generation, a royal priesthood, a holy nation, His own special people, that you may proclaim the praises of Him who called you out of darkness into His marvellous light; who once were not a people but are now the people of God." This family is spread across the whole world and is made up of every culture and language. It is not limited to a building, just as a natural family isn't limited to their house.

So how do you get connected in this family?

As a Christian, you are automatically part of God's large family, called the Universal Church, but He also has a smaller family for you to be a part of, called a local church. It's like having relatives all over the world, but living with your immediate family. The Bible says, "God settles the solitary in a home; He leads out the prisoners to prosperity, but the rebellious dwell in a parched land" (Psalm 68:6). A local church is just a group of believers in Jesus who have committed to support each other and follow Jesus together. You may or may not belong to a local church right now, and there is still a bit to learn about it all, but take a moment now and just thank God for adopting you in His family and having a great plan for you.

Journal any thoughts below:

Scriptures

"How good and pleasant it is when brothers live together in unity!" **Psalm 133: 1**

"Those who accept his message were baptized, and able three thousand were added to their number that day." **Acts 2:41**

"All the believers were one in heart and mind. No one claimed that any of his possessions was his own, but they shared everything they had." **Acts 4:32**

According to the Bible, what is the church?

Are you currently a part of a local church or group of believers?

a. Yes

b. Not yet

Why did God create the Church to be like a family?

Why did God create the Church to be like a family?

Right from the start, Jesus made His followers as special as His own mom and siblings. "Pointing to his disciples, [Jesus] said, "Here are my mother and my brothers. For whoever does the will of my Father in heaven is my brother and sister and mother" (Matthew 12:49,50). That is why we can call each other "brothers" and "sisters" in Christ.

Think about all the benefits of a family.

A family provides a warm, safe place for you to call home. It gives you your sense of security and identity, and teaches you the difference between right and wrong. Your family feeds and clothes you. It is in a family that you learn how to love your siblings and respect your parents. And it is in a family that you discover who you are and how you can contribute to the world.

God wants you to have a spiritual family in a local church. A young baby can't be expected to feed himself, change his diaper, and teach himself all the things he needs to know as an adult. Just the same, God knows you need the guidance of a pastor, the care of other Christians, and the safety and support of a good church home to help you grow as a Christian. Listen to what the Bible says about it: Two are better than one, because they have a good return for their work: If one falls down, his friend can help him up. But pity the man who falls and has no one to help him up! Also, if two lie down together, they will keep warm. But how can one keep warm alone? Though one may be overpowered, two can defend themselves. A cord of three strands is not quickly broken" (Ecclesiastes 4:9-12). Take a moment and ask God to lead you to the right church, if you don't yet have one. And if you do, ask God to speak to you about the church family you do have and how you can contribute.

Journal any thoughts below:

Scriptures

"And let us consider how to stimulate one another to love and good deeds, not forsaking our own assembling together as in the habit of some, but encouraging one another; and all the more as you see the day drawing near." **Hebrews 10:24-25**

"I was glad when they said to me, 'Let us go to the house of the LORD." **Psalm 122:1**

"And all those who had believed were together and had all things in common." **Acts 2:44**

Why did God create the Church to be like a family?

How connected are you to other Christians?

a. Very

b. Some

c. Little

d. None

So how does the Church Work?

So how does the Church work?

Jesus said, "I will build My Church, and the gates of Hades will not overpower it" (Matthew 16:18). But how is Jesus building His Church? Ephesians 4:16 tells us the answer: "As each part does its own special work, it helps the other parts grow." Did you know that you are meant to play a crucial part in God's family?

Imagine for a moment a young boy who never wanted anything to do with his family.

He never came out for family dinner, but just ran in his room when he got home from school. He never did any chores around the house, refused to clean his room, and pushed his brother whenever he saw him. In addition, this boy had it in him to become a great soccer player, but he never let his dad teach him how to play. Think of all that child would miss out on! Not to mention how the family would suffer as well.

Just like a family, the church has a give-and-take relationship—like how people need the oxygen trees give off and trees need the carbon dioxide people breathe out. Just the same, you need the Church, and the church also needs you. Look at mutual benefits of being in a church:

You are protected: Just as a house keeps people protected from harm, so God's house keeps Christians safe from false teaching. God gave this instruction to pastors: "So guard yourselves and God's people. Feed and shepherd God's flock—his church, purchased with his own blood—over which the Holy Spirit has appointed you as elders" (Acts 20:28).

You are taught how to follow Jesus: I Peter 2:2,3 says, "Like newborn babies, you must crave pure spiritual milk so that you will grow into a full experience of salvation. Cry out for this nourishment, now that you have had a taste of the Lord's kindness." Newborns can't feed themselves; they need someone to help them. Pastors and teachers help you grow as a Christian as they feed you the spiritual food of the Bible and help you know God better.

You learn how to love your family: Jesus said, "So now I am giving you a new commandment: Love each other. Just as I have loved you, you should love each other. Your love for one another will prove to the world that you are my disciples" (John 13:34,35). Being part of a church family helps you learn how to love others and their differences and show the love of Jesus to the world.

You discover and use your gifts: Have you ever had someone tell you that you are good at something you were unaware of? God has given you spiritual gifts, and your church family can help you discover them and learn how to use them. The Bible says, "Since you want spiritual gifts very much, seek most of all to have the gifts that help the church grow stronger" (I Corinthians 14:12). As you use your gifts, the church is strengthened and grows.

You need the Church and the Church needs you. What are the gifts God has given you to build His Church? Maybe you haven't discovered them yet. As you join a spiritual family, you grow as a Christian and help the whole body of Christ to grow as well.

Journal any thoughts below:

Scriptures

"They were continually devoting themselves to the apostles'
teaching and to fellowship, to the breaking of bread and to prayer."
Acts 2:42

"Day by day continuing with one mind in the temple, and breaking
bread from house to house, they were taking their meals together
with gladness and sincerity of heart." **Acts 2:46**

"Therefore encourage one another and build up one another, just as
you also are doing." **I Thessalonians 5:11**

How can you use the gifts God has given you to build the local
church?

Are you aware of any of your spiritual gifts?

a. Very

b. Some

c. Little

d. None

How to Find a Good Church

What Makes a Good Church? We've talked a lot about church being like a family…so how do you find the right one? Not every church is perfect—in fact, no church is perfect just like no family is perfect. You may be in a part of the world where there are no organized local churches; if that is the case pray that God will lead you to some other Christians that you can have fellowship with. If there are churches near where you live, you should pray and ask God for His wisdom to help you find the one He wants you to go to. Here are some questions to help guide you in your search for a church that is good for you.

* **Does it believe that faith in Jesus is the only way to be saved from your sins and have a relationship with God?** "It is by grace you have been saved through faith. And this not from yourselves; it is the gift of God, not by works, that no one should boast" (Ephesians 2:8,9). Some churches teach "extra" things you have to do to be saved—that faith in Jesus alone isn't quite enough. This is a major red flag.

* Does it believe that the Bible is 100% true and try to live it out on a daily basis? Jesus said, "Blessed rather are those who hear the word of God and obey it" (Luke 11:28). Some churches only believe certain parts of the Bible or have added extra books to it. This is not good. You want a church that respects the Bible as God's word and as the guidebook for life.

* Does it seek to tell the world around them about Jesus and be an example of God's kingdom on earth? "Then Jesus came to them and said, 'All authority in heaven and on earth has been given to me. Therefore go and make disciples of all nations, baptizing them in the name of the Father and of the Son and of the Holy Spirit, and teaching them to obey everything I have commanded you'" (Matthew 28:18-20). It can be easy to get inwardly focused in a church and lose the driving mission of telling others about Jesus' salvation. But that is the purpose of every church. So, find one that is actively obeying Jesus' command to preach the gospel and love others.

If you can find a church with these things, praise God! Each church will have a different "personality," just as families do. Maybe they sing different songs than you're used to or have different ways to reach out to their community. But what really matters is the core beliefs about Jesus and commitment to follow Him. Do you have a church that matches these qualities? If so, thank God and ask Him how you can serve there. But if not, take a moment to ask God to lead you to one. He has promised to provide for you, so you can trust Him to answer your request.

Journal any thoughts below:

Scriptures

"But as the church is subject to Christ, so also the wives ought to be to their husbands in everything." **Ephesians 5:24**

"Now we command you, brethren in the name of our Lord Jesus Christ, that you keep away from every brother who leads an unruly life not according to the tradition which you received from us." **2 Thessalonians 3:6**

"Whoever then annuls one of the least of these commandments, and teaches others to do the same, shall be called least in the kingdom of heaven; but whoever keeps and teaches them, he shall be called great in the kingdom of heaven." **Matthew 5:19**

Out of all the things you've learned about the Church from these lessons, which ones mean the most to you?

How often are you attending church or meeting with a small group of Christians?

a. Seldom

b. One or two times a month

c. Weekly

How to Be Involved in Church

What should you do when you go to Church? If you know someone already at church, they can help guide you to activities that would be good for you. If at all possible it is good if you can go to church services each Sunday. Many churches have Bible studies or small groups that meet to study God's Word; if so these can be a great help to you. You can also begin to help and serve others, even if you are just a very new Christian; maybe there are ways to minister to others at your church.

The Church is Jesus' own body on the earth. The Bible says, "God has put all things under the authority of Christ and has made him head over all things for the benefit of the church. And the church is his body; it is made full and complete by Christ, who fills all things everywhere with Himself" (Ephesians 1:22,23). That's what the Bible says, but what does that mean? Think of your own body. Your head tells the rest of your body what to do. If you want your arm to pick something up, it does it. If you want to step on something, your foot obeys the command. It is the same with the Church. We are the representatives of who Jesus is and what He wants done in the world. That means, when people ask the question, "Who is Jesus?", they can look to the Church and find their answers.

This is a wonderful responsibility. Being Jesus' body means we act like He acts and tell others about Him. The Bible asks this question, "How can people have faith in the Lord and ask him to save them, if they have never heard about him? And how can they hear, unless someone tells them? And how can anyone tell them without being sent by the Lord?" (Romans 10:14,15). This is the main goal of the Church—to tell others about Jesus that they too may be saved and added to God's family. You have an important role to play your part. Maybe God gave you the gift of singing so that you can sing about Him to others. Or maybe He made you to be a teacher and teach people about Jesus. Whatever role God has made you to play is a very crucial one, and His body cannot function at its best without you.

Journal any thoughts below:

Scriptures

"And each day the Lord was adding to their number day by day those who were being saved." **Acts 2:47**

"And when they prayed, the place where they had gathered together was shaken, and they were all filled with the Holy Spirit and began to speak the word of God with boldness." **Acts 4:31**

"And with great power the apostles were giving testimony to the resurrection of the Lord Jesus, and abundant grace was upon them all." **Acts 4:33**

What do you see as the purpose of the Church?

Do you feel personally included in Jesus' command to tell the world about Him and make disciples in all nations?

a. Very

b. Some

c. Little

d. None

6

SHARING YOUR FAITH

Great Commission 101

How did you first hear about Jesus? Someone told you right? It is very rare for someone to have heard about Jesus just through a dream or message from God. For most people, they had to hear it from someone. Romans 10:14,15 says, "How can people have faith in the Lord and ask Him to save them, if they have never heard about him? And how can they hear, unless someone tells them? And how can anyone tell them without being sent by the Lord?" Did you know that you have been sent by the Lord to tell people the good news about Jesus and how they can be forgiven of their sins?

This amazing task is called the Great Commission. It's what Jesus told His followers right before He left earth to go to Heaven. He said, "I have been given all authority in heaven and on earth! Go to the people of all nations and make them my disciples. Baptize them in the name of the Father, the Son, and the Holy Spirit, and teach them to do everything I have told you. I will be with you always, even until the end of the world" (Matthew 28:18-20). As one of Jesus' followers, you have the privilege and the responsibility of helping to fulfil the Great Commission. The goal is that every single person on earth would be given the chance to hear about Jesus that they might receive eternal life as you have.

Think of it this way: Imagine you had cancer and were chosen to be part of a special test group for a new cure. The treatment cured all of your cancer completely free of charge. What is the first thing you would do after you were healed? You would want to tell all of the other cancer victims about this great cure! Well, sin is a cancer affecting every single person. And you been cured—forgiven of your sins—by Jesus Christ. Do you remember how you felt before you believed in Jesus? Maybe you felt lonely, guilty, and without hope. The entire world is lost with Jesus. That is why Jesus has sent us to reach them with His love and forgiveness. Will you obey His command to make disciples of all nations? If so, tell God right now that you desire to give your life to this. It is the greatest thing you can do with your life.

Journal any thoughts below:

Scriptures

"Believe in the Lord Jesus, and you will be saved, you and your household." **Acts 16:31**

"And He has made from one man every nation of mankind to live on all the face of the earth, having determined their appointed times and the boundaries of their habitation, that they would seek God, if perhaps they might grope for Him and find Him, though He is not far from each of us." **Acts 17:26,27**

"And He ordered us to preach to the people, and solemnly to testify that this is the One who has been appointed by God as Judge of the living and the dead." **Acts 11:42**

What can I do to tell more people about Jesus?

How often have you shared your faith with others?

a. Never

b. Once or twice

c. Three times or more

Why Share?

Have you ever bet on something?

It's easy to make a bet when the stakes are low, say, buying dinner or doing the dishes. But what if the stakes are high? What if the cost of losing the bet would totally change your life? When it comes to the Great Commission, the stakes are very high—life and death, to be specific. Have you ever met a Christian who seemed a little too radical? Maybe they couldn't stop talking about Jesus...maybe they even were a little embarrassing? Paul was so radical that even when he was put in jail for talking about Jesus, he only cared about the gospel being preached. He said, "My dear friends, I want you to know that what has happened to me has helped to spread the good news. The Roman guards and all the others know that I am here in jail because I serve Christ. Now most of the Lord's followers have become brave and are fearlessly telling the message" (Philippians 1:12-14). Why was Paul willing to risk his life for the sake of the message about Jesus being told?

It is because life and death are at stake.

The only way for someone to be saved from sin and receive eternal life is through faith in Jesus. There is no other way. "Jesus answered, 'I am the way and the truth and the life. No one comes to the Father except through me'" (John 14:6). So, if someone doesn't hear about Jesus, they face eternity in hell. And Jesus has entrusted the job to us—His followers. That is why Paul didn't care about being put in jail, about being beaten, made fun of, excluded, and eventually killed for the gospel. He knew everything he went through would be worth people being saved from their sins. Have you ever run a race before? You have to train your body with long, hard hours of exercise and give up certain foods and activities to be in the best shape. But the end goal of winning the race makes it worth it. If you can understand the eternal difference you preaching the gospel can make in other's lives, it will drive you to sacrifice great things for it. Ask God right now to help you understand what is at stake eternally and how you can make a difference.

Journal any thoughts below:

Scriptures

"For we cannot stop speaking about what we have seen and heard."
Acts 4: 20

"For the wages of sin is death, but the free gift of God is eternal life
in Christ Jesus our Lord." **Romans 6:23**

"Death and life are in the power of the tongue, and those who love it
will eat its fruit." **Proverbs 18:21**

Why was Paul willing to risk his life for the sake of the gospel
message?

How willing are you to share your faith?

a. Very

b. Some

c. Little

d. None

What is the Gospel Anyway?

If someone asked you how to get to heaven, would you know what to tell them?

When I was a young girl, my mom drove me to my friend's house almost everyday for 5 years. But if someone had asked me how to get to her house, I couldn't tell them, because I had never driven there myself. A lot of Christians feel that way with the gospel. They generally know what it means to be a Christian, but if someone asked them how to become one, they wouldn't know what to say. I Peter 3:15 says, "Always be ready to answer everyone who asks you to explain about the hope you have." You don't have to have been a Christian for many years or be a preacher to share the gospel; you just need to be willing. Bill Bright described successful evangelism as "taking the initiative to share the gospel in the power of the Holy Spirit and leaving the results to God." But what exactly is the gospel?

The Gospel is the good news about Jesus Christ coming to earth to save us from our sins.

That's it. Nothing more, nothing less. If you can tell someone one thing, tell them about Jesus. Speaking of Him, the Bible says, "You can't be saved by believing in anyone else. God has given us no other name under heaven that will save us" (Acts 4:12). Tell them that Jesus is God, who came to earth as a man, and died for the sins of the world. Tell them that they can be completely forgiven of their sins and receive eternal life with God solely by believing in Jesus as Savior and Lord. The Bible gives everyone this guarantee: "If you confess with your mouth the Lord Jesus and believe in your heart that God has raised Him from the dead, you will be saved" (Romans 10:9). That is the gospel. Anyone can share it and everyone needs to hear it. Pray and ask God for an opportunity this week to share the gospel. Remember: all you need to do is take the initiative to share the gospel in the power of the Holy Spirit and leave the results to God.

Journal any thoughts below:

Scriptures

"And there is salvation in no one else; for there is no other name under heaven that has been given among men by which we must be saved." **Acts 4:12**

"For by grace you have been saved, through faith; and that not of yourselves, it is the gift of God; not as a result of works, so that no one may boast." **Ephesians 2:8,9**

"For God did not send His Son into the world to judge the world, but that the world might be saved through Him." **John 3:17**

How can I explain to someone else that faith in Jesus Christ is the only way to be saved?

How confident are you in leading someone to Christ?

a. Very

b. Some

c. Little

d. None

How Do I Share the Gospel?

There are many ways you can share your faith with others. The first and most important thing to do is to pray for the person you want to share with. (If you live in a country where you can be persecuted for your faith you should ask God for wisdom in how you proceed.) Then you can ask God to open the door to have a conversation with them. When you talk to them, you can ask them whether they are interested in spiritual things, or whether have accepted Christ as their Savior. There are booklets that you can use that will tell someone about Jesus Christ; one great one is the Four Spiritual Laws from Campus Crusade for Christ. You can read through the booklet with the person and at the end ask them if they would like to accept Jesus Christ as their Savior. The important thing is to tell them that God loves them; that Jesus Christ died for their sins; and that they can accept Jesus Christ as their Savior if they want by praying and asking forgiveness of their sins and asking Jesus into their hearts.

If someone does not live near you, you can also send them an email that tells them about your new faith in Jesus Christ. In the email you can provide a link to an evangelistic website like **www.4StepstoGod.com** or another one that God used in your life. You can send emails to many of your friends or send them a

Christian book or pamphlet. You can also ask God for His love to shine through you to others. There may be practical ways that you can display God's love to others as you look for opportunities to tell others about Jesus. Whatever you do, you can ask God for boldness in telling others about Jesus.

Who needs to hear about the gospel? And who needs to tell it? The same answer is for both questions. Everyone. Every person on earth needs to hear the gospel and every Christian needs to tell them. It's not the job of pastors or preachers. "And He [Jesus] said to them [His followers], 'Go into all the world, and preach the Gospel to all creation.'" (Mark 16:15). If you are a follower of Christ, you have been told to go and preach the gospel. Imagine you lived in a desert where everyone around you was dying of thirst. You were the only one who knew where an unlimited water supply was…who would you tell? Everyone right? And you would probably start with the person closest to you. After you told them and they drank the water, you would instruct them to tell others as you continued to do the same. This would get the job done in the shortest amount of time and make sure everyone got some water. It's the same the Great Commission.

Everyone is spiritually dying of thirst. And you know where the water is, since you have tasted it. Jesus answered, "Everyone who drinks this water will thirst again; but whoever drinks of the water that I will give him will become in him a well of water springing up to eternal life." (John 4:13,14). Do you know someone who is spiritually thirsty? Maybe they have been trying to fill their thirst in a job, relationship, or possessions. But they keep ending up thirsty. You do not need to look very far to find someone who is desperate to hear about Jesus. Chances are your neighbour, family member, or co-worker is waiting for someone to tell them there is a way to be forgiven of their sin. YOU are that person. You do not need to be a preacher or Bible expert; you just need to care and be willing to share the good news about Jesus. Take this great adventure with the Holy Spirit to lead people to salvation! Ask God to make you bold to share the gospel with the many thirsty people around you.

Journal any thoughts below:

Scriptures

"And when they had prayed, the place where they had gathered together was shaken, and they were all filled with the Holy Spirit and began to speak the word of God with boldness." **Acts 4:31**

"He said to them, 'Go into all the world and preach the gospel to all creation. He who has believed and has been baptized shall be saved; but he who has disbelieved shall be condemned." **Mark 16:15,16**

"Go therefore and make disciples of all the nations, baptizing them in the name of the Father and the Son and the Holy Spirit." **Matthew 28:19**

Have you asked God to make you bold to share the gospel with those who need to hear?

How willing are you to boldly share the gospel?

a. Very

b. Some

c. Little

d. None

Don't be Scared

You're not alone. Breathe a sigh of relief. This is not God sending you out on your own to preach the gospel all over the world and saying, "Good luck!" No, He has promised to send the Holy Spirit to help you be an effective witness for Jesus Christ. Jesus said, "But the Helper, the Holy Spirit, whom the Father will send in My name, He will teach you all things, and bring to your remembrance all that I said to you." (John 14:26). What does it mean that the Holy Spirit is your Helper to be a witness for Jesus?

Imagine a sailboat. You set out to sail across the sea to another country. You buy your boat, map out your general direction, and take off from land. But you have to trust that the wind is going to come, fill your sails, and carry your boat across the sea. That's a lot like witnessing. You have heard the command from Jesus to go and make disciples of all nations. You can set your heart to be obedient to Him and prepare to tell others about Jesus, but it's the Holy Spirit who is going to fill your sails and do all the work. And He promises to send the wind to you. Jesus said, "but you will receive power when the Holy Spirit has come upon you; and you shall be My witnesses" (Acts 1:8).

And it doesn't matter if you don't have a naturally "bold" personality. Sometimes we think that only the really confident or outgoing people are good at sharing the gospel. But the power of the Holy Spirit is available for everyone—not just the extroverts. Think of the sailboat illustration: it doesn't matter if the sailboat is big, small, brown, colorful, long, or short. As long as it has sails, the wind can carry it. It's the same with the Holy Spirit: He can take whatever personality you have and use it to draw fame and glory to Jesus. The sails of your boat are just your willingness to tell others about Jesus. The Holy Spirit will give you the power and the right words. Would you like to witness with the help of the Holy Spirit? Ask God right not to fill you with His Spirit and give you opportunities to witness. Jesus said, "How much more will your Heavenly Father give the Holy Spirit to those whoask Him!" (Luke 11:13). As you and the Holy Spirit work together, you will see people believe in Jesus and receive eternal life.

Journal any thoughts below:

Scriptures

"But sanctify Christ as Lord in your hearts, always being ready to make a defence to everyone who asks you to give an account for the hope that is in you, yet with gentleness and reverence." **1 Peter 3:15**

"How then will they call on Him in whom they have not believed? How will they believe in Him whom they have not heard? And how will they hear without a preacher?" **Romans 10:14**

"For I am not ashamed of the gospel, for it is the power of God for salvation to everyone who believes, to the Jew first and also to the Greek." **Romans 1:16**

 What do you need to do to get over the fear of sharing your faith with others?

Based on what you have learned in these lessons, how confident are you about sharing the gospel?

a. Very

b. Some

c. Little

d. None

Congratulations on completing the thirty lessons

The Apostle John tells us that what "you have heard, what you have seen with your eyes and what you have held in our hands concerning the Word of Life" bears witness and proclaims the eternal life we have through Jesus Christ. We have good news to share with those around us.